A young *explorer* meets a chipmunk in his backyard.

The World
Beneath Your Feet

by Judith E. Rinard

☐ BOOKS FOR YOUNG EXPLORERS
☐ NATIONAL GEOGRAPHIC SOCIETY

This forest is cool, green, and quiet. Soft moss covers the rocks. Nothing seems to move. But look under flowers, stones, and logs. You might find a whole world of plants and animals— right at your feet!

A snail glides slowly along the ground.
It leaves a slimy trail. The snail has
eyes at the tips of the long stalks on its head.
It can stretch an eye and see over a leaf.

A dead log is a home for many living things. What might you see if you come very close? This turtle looks big, but it is only as long as your foot. How many other animals can you find? Insects live in the wood. Snakes, toads, and birds eat the insects. As the wood rots, it slowly becomes new soil. Wildflowers and other plants grow in the rich soil. Under the log, small animals find cool hiding places.

Look for the names of these plants and animals in the back of this book.

Among the moss and ferns, some animals find food. Two box turtles are looking for berries, leaves, and snails. A box turtle has a hard shell that protects it from enemies. When it is alarmed, the turtle pulls itself inside. It closes the shell so tightly that a hungry animal cannot open it.

American toad

Box turtles

Pickerel frog

Listen! In spring, you can hear a male toad call. Its throat fills with air and helps make the sound loud. A frog may catch an insect under the leaves.

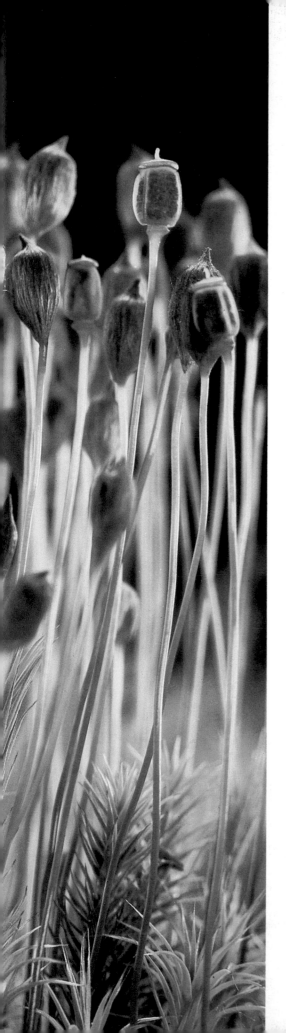

Do you see the little toad sitting in a forest
of moss? This young toad is so small
it could easily sit on your fingertip.
All around the toad are the green leaves
and brown stalks of the moss plant.

At the tops of the stalks are capsules.
They are full of spores, which are a little like
very tiny seeds. When the capsules open,
the spores spill out like grains of pepper
from a shaker. New moss plants may grow
where the wind blows the spores.

Common toad in hair-cap moss

9

Many kinds of plants grow
on the forest floor in spring.
How do you think
the skunk cabbage got its name?

Jack-in-the-pulpit

Puffball

Skunk cabbage

Jack-in-the-pulpit blooms in spring. Can you see "Jack" standing
in his pulpit? In fall, you might see a plant called a puffball.
Press it, and whoosh! Out comes a cloud of spores. Mushrooms spring up
in damp soil. Look at them, but don't touch! Some are poisonous.

Mushrooms

Blue Ridge red salamander under reindeer lichen (LY-kun)

If you walk beside
a stream, you may see
a salamander near the
water. This one is creeping
out from under a plant
called reindeer lichen.
This salamander is about
as long as a teaspoon.

Its skin can dry out easily.
The salamander must stay
in a cool, moist place.

In the daytime,
salamanders hide in moss,
under stones, or in wet
earth. In the evening, they
come out and hunt for
snails, insects, and worms.

Outside the forest, a little vole hides in a field of clover. It spends much of its time running around, looking for food and eating. It makes runways in the grass. An earthworm is crawling out of the ground near some blades of grass. Spotted ladybugs busily hunt for tiny insects on a dandelion flower. The yellow flower will soon become a fluffy white ball of seeds.

Spotted ladybugs on dandelion

Meadow vole in clover

Earthworm

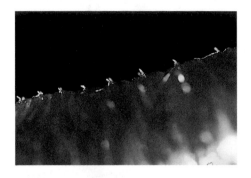

If you dig into the
ground with a shovel,
you may see the tunnels
that earthworms make.

The worms loosen the soil.
This helps plants grow.
Through tunnels made
by earthworms, air and
rainwater get to the
roots of plants.

An earthworm has tiny
bristles on its skin
that help it move.
You can feel them
if you run your finger
gently over an earthworm.

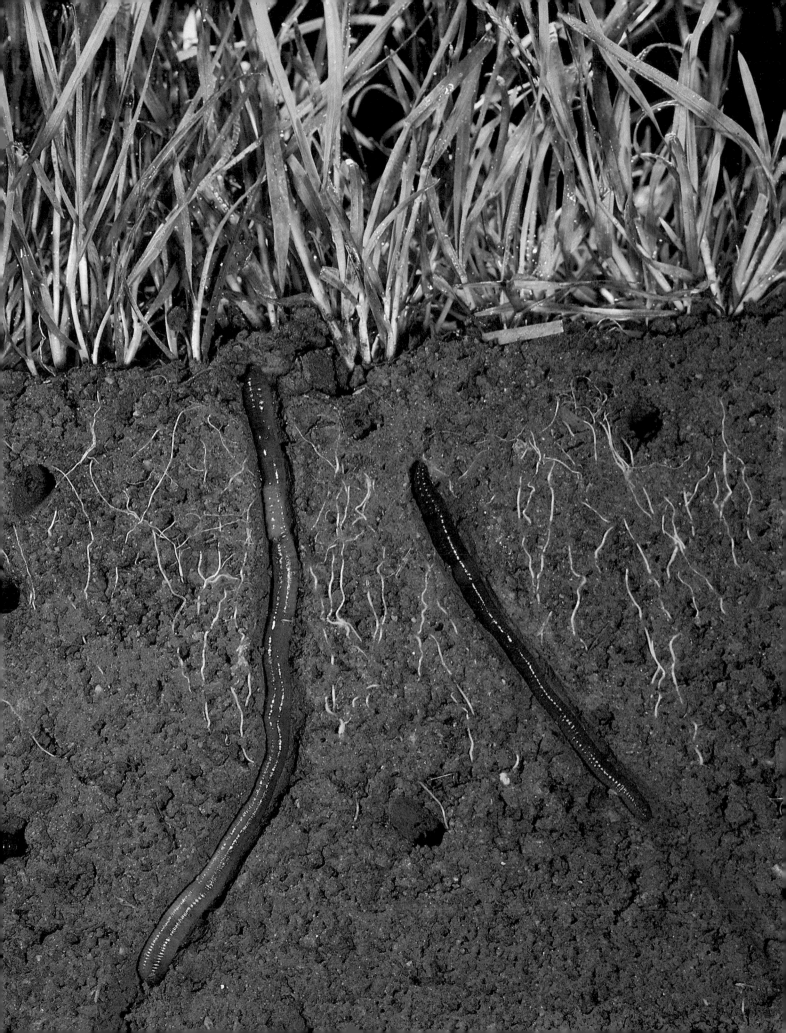

There is a lot going on below the ground you walk on. If you could peek underground, you might see some of these animals. Moles and worms make tunnels in the dirt. Baby voles, still pink and hairless, curl up near their mother. A chipmunk takes a nap in its cozy nest. Above the ground, a shrew has caught a worm.
A screech owl is looking for something to eat.
What do you think it might find?

Lodgepole chipmunk

Safe in her underground home, a mother chipmunk cares for her babies. She gently carries one in her mouth.

Born without hair, the babies will begin to grow fur in about ten days. Newborn chipmunks cannot see.

In about six weeks, they will be big enough to leave the burrow and explore the world above the ground.

Star-nosed mole

Wiggling its feelers, a star-nosed mole comes out of a dark tunnel. The 22 pink feelers on its nose help the mole find food. It cannot see very well. It feels a worm moving by and grabs it, quick as a wink.

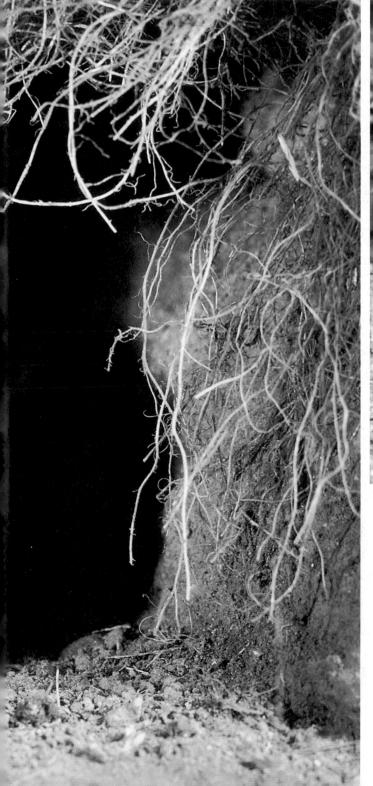

The star-nosed mole lives
in damp or muddy soil.
It is a good swimmer.
It hunts in streams for
water insects and small fish.

Like a little bulldozer, a common mole pushes dirt aside. This kind of mole looks different from the star-nosed mole. A common mole has a long pointed snout. Can you find its eyes? The mole's tiny eyes are hidden in its thick fur. Like the star-nosed mole, it is almost blind.

Moles have short strong legs and long wide claws. They are good diggers and can tunnel fast. You may never see moles, for they stay mainly under the ground. But you might see hills of loose dirt in your yard. Moles make these as they dig.

Eastern American mole

Some kinds of spiders live under the ground, too.
During the day, a wolf spider rests under logs or stones or in a burrow.
It comes out at night and hunts for insects on the forest floor.
This mother wolf spider is carrying her babies on her back.

Wolf spider carrying young

The trap-door spider uses its underground home to trap small insects.
It digs a narrow tunnel and lines it with silk from its body.
Then it makes a little door that it can open and close.
The spider waits in the tunnel. When an insect goes by the door,
the spider pops out and grabs it.

Trap-door spider

Black-tailed prairie dog

Black-footed ferret

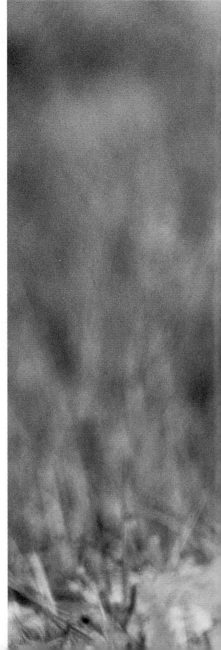

Burrowing owls

Prairie dogs build towns under the ground. Other animals share them. Outside its burrow, a young prairie dog kisses a parent.

Below ground, young owls huddle together. When a prairie dog family moves out of its home, burrowing owls may move right in. Under the ground, these animals can hide from a hawk, a coyote, or a fox.

A hungry black-footed ferret will follow prairie dogs into their tunnels. But the ferret has enemies, too. It may run underground if a coyote comes near. The ferret also raises its young in a prairie dog town.

From the safety of its burrow, a prairie dog watches for danger. Many creatures make their homes in the world beneath your feet. When you go exploring, leave their homes as you find them.

Published by The National Geographic Society, Washington, D. C.

Gilbert M. Grosvenor, *President*
Melvin M. Payne, *Chairman of the Board*
Owen R. Anderson, *Executive Vice President*
Robert L. Breeden, *Vice President, Publications and Educational Media*

Prepared by The Special Publications Division

Donald J. Crump, *Director*
Philip B. Silcott, *Associate Director*
William L. Allen, *Assistant Director*

Staff for this book

Jane H. Buxton, *Managing Editor*
Jim Abercrombie, *Picture Editor*
Jody Bolt, *Art Director*
Rebecca Lescaze, *Researcher*
Peggy D. Winston, *Assistant Researcher*
Robert Hynes, *Contributing Artist*
Pamela J. Castaldi, *Assistant Designer*
Artemis S. Lampathakis, *Illustrations Assistant*
Elizabeth Ann Brazerol, Dianne T. Craven, Carol R. Curtis,
    Mary Elizabeth Davis, Eva Dillon, Rosamund Garner, Annie Hampford,
    Virginia W. Hannasch, Cleo Petroff, Pamela Black Townsend,
    Virginia A. Williams, Eric Wilson, *Staff Assistants*

Engraving, Printing, and Product Manufacture

Robert W. Messer, *Manager*
George V. White, *Production Manager*
George J. Zeller, *Production Project Manager*
Mark R. Dunlevy, David V. Showers, Gregory Storer, *Assistant
    Production Managers;* Mary A. Bennett, *Production Assistant;*
    Julia F. Warner, *Production Staff Assistant*

Consultants

Lynda Bush, *Reading Consultant*
Peter L. Munroe, *Educational Consultant*
Dr. Nicholas J. Long, *Consulting Psychologist*
Dr. Ronald M. Nowak, Office of Endangered Species,
    U. S. Fish and Wildlife Service; Ronald I. Crombie,
    Division of Amphibians and Reptiles, Smithsonian Institution;
    Dr. Robert O. Petty, Professor of Biology, Wabash College,
    Scientific Consultants

Illustrations Credits

ANIMALS ANIMALS/Z. Leszczynski (cover, 6-7); ANIMALS ANIMALS/Joe
McDonald (3 upper); National Geographic Photographer James P. Blair
(2-3); Rod Planck/TOM STACK & ASSOCIATES (7 upper); Harry Ellis (7
lower, 10 lower right, 12-13, 15 right); Jane Burton/BRUCE COLEMAN
INC. (8-9); Marilyn Wood/PHOTO/NATS (10 left); Ray Elliott, Jr. (10
upper right); Ralph Hunt Williams (10-11); John Serrao (14-15); Hans
Pfletschinger/PETER ARNOLD, INC. (15 left, 16); Jean-Paul
Ferrero/ARDEA LONDON LTD. (16-17); Tom McHugh/PHOTO
RESEARCHERS, INC. (20-21); Dwight R. Kuhn/BRUCE COLEMAN INC.
(22-23); Dwight R. Kuhn (23, 26); Leonard Lee Rue III (24-25 all); Paul
A. Zahl, Ph.D. (27); François Gohier/ARDEA LONDON LTD. (28 upper);
R. Allin/BRUCE COLEMAN INC. (28 lower); Franz J. Camenzind (28-29);
Jim Brandenburg (30-31); Breck P. Kent (32).

Library of Congress CIP Data
Rinard, Judith E.
    The world beneath your feet.
    (Books for young explorers)
    Summary: Describes briefly the characteristics of the various animals that live underneath
the soil.
    1. Soil biology—Juvenile literature.   [1. Soil biology]   I. Title.   II. Series.
QH84.8.R56   1985   591.909'4   85-13642
ISBN   0-87044-561-8 (regular edition)
ISBN   0-87044-566-9 (library edition)

Almost out of sight, a spadefoot toad
digs backward into the sand. This kind
of toad lives in dry places. It digs so
quickly with its hind feet that it seems
to sink into the soil. It spends most
of its time below ground. On cool rainy
evenings, it comes out to hunt insects.

COVER: A striped chipmunk fills
its cheek pouches with nuts.
Chipmunks store nuts and seeds
for winter in their underground homes.

MORE ABOUT

All around us—in fields and forests, along the banks of streams and ponds, and even in your own backyard—there exist small worlds of plant and animal life. Many animals live in communities at the surface and under the ground. They spend much of their lives out of our sight, so we are hardly aware of them. But by carefully observing and listening, we can discover these creatures and learn much about their habits.

A forest floor is full of life. Look for plants, such as mosses, ferns, mushrooms, and wildflowers (2-3, 6-7, 8-9, 10-11).* They offer shelter and hiding

places for a great many animals, including chipmunks, snails, frogs, toads, insects, and spiders (1, 3, 7, 8-9, 26-27). Often these animals blend so well with their surroundings that you cannot see them at first, although they are just a few feet away from you.

But look closely at and under a rotting log (4-5). It may appear to be a lifeless object, but you will find that it holds a microcosm of animal life.

If you roll aside a rock, you will discover another miniature world of life. Like the log, the rock blocks out sunlight and holds in moisture, creating a cool,

damp, and dark environment. Here, animals that cannot endure the drying heat of the sun thrive. For example, slugs, a kind of snail, and salamanders (12-13) dry out very easily. So these animals often hide during the day and come out at night.

Insects lay their eggs and build homes under rocks and logs. Look for ants, ground beetles, and wood roaches. You may also spot the lizards and spiders that feed on insects.

Some wolf spiders dig burrows under rocks, where they rest during the day (26). The wolf spider gets its name from its way of hunting food. It does not construct a web to catch its prey. Instead, it stalks and chases down its victim and kills it with a bite.

The forest floor is covered with litter—dead leaves, twigs, seeds, empty shells and skins, and other decaying plant and animal matter. All this material is slowly converted, with the aid of microscopic organisms, into a dark substance called humus. Humus mixes with bits of crushed rock to become rich new soil.

Earthworms in the soil act as natural plows, making passageways for air and water (16-17). In their burrows, worms feed on dead leaves (15). Fibers in the leaves pass through the worms and become new earth. As the earthworms move, they mix and churn the soil. All this activity helps plants grow.

Earthworms have many tiny hooklike bristles on their bodies called setae. These serve as "feet" to help the worms crawl through soil.

As you walk in the woods near the edge of a field, look for holes under old tree

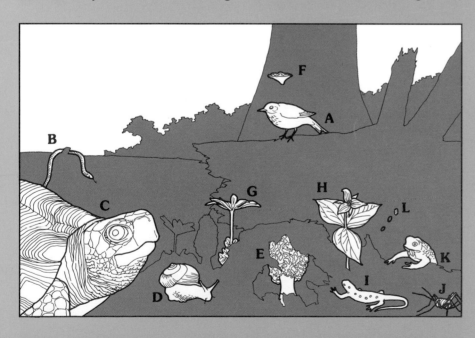

This drawing provides a key to the painting on pages 4-5 in the book. It shows more creatures than would normally gather at one time. On top of the log perches a thrush (**A**), watching for insects to eat. A black rat snake (**B**) slides along looking for birds and their eggs, lizards, and mice. A box turtle (**C**) crawls near to feed on mushrooms. A snail (**D**) searches for plant leaves. Plants growing on or near the log include sponge mushrooms (**E**); shelf or bracket fungi (**F**); and two wildflowers, bloodroot (**G**) and wake-robin (**H**). A red eft (**I**) and a camel cricket (**J**) look for shady hiding places. A Fowler's toad (**K**) catches an insect. Sow bugs (**L**) feed on the decaying log.

*Numbers in parentheses refer to pages in
The World Beneath Your Feet.

stumps or large rocks. These may be the entrances to chipmunks' homes.

Chipmunks are small members of the squirrel family. Some dig tunnels leading to various rooms for sleeping, raising young (20-21), eating, and storing food. These animals sleep in their burrows at night and during the cold winter months (18-19). You are most likely to see chipmunks in the late summer and fall, when they busily scurry about, gathering nuts and seeds to store for winter (front cover).

In meadows, in parks, or in your own backyard, look for other small animals. Among the most numerous are insects. On a hot summer day or night, you can hear the buzzing, chirping, and humming of a chorus of bees, crickets, and grasshoppers.

Another animal you might find there is the vole (18). Like a tiny lawnmower, this rodent cuts little pathways through the grass and clover with its teeth (14-15). Plants covering their runways help hide voles from predators such as owls and house cats. Running down the paths, voles look for seeds, leaves, insects, and bumblebees' eggs to eat. Voles spend most of their time hunting for food and eating.

In grassy areas, you might also see the telltale signs of moles, especially on golfcourses and lawns and in fields. As moles dig near the surface, they make ridges of upturned earth.

The eastern American, or common, mole is only about seven inches long. Yet this little animal can tunnel at about 15 feet an hour. An expert digger, the mole uses the long, flat claws of its powerful front feet to scratch out dirt (18-19, 24-25). Its velvety fur will lie flat in the direction the mole is moving. This helps it slip through narrow tunnels as it hunts earthworms and insects.

A number of burrowing animals, including the prairie dog (28-29), live on the open grasslands, where there are very few trees for the animals to hide

behind. Their safest refuge from predators such as coyotes, foxes, hawks, eagles, and bobcats is underground.

Black-tailed prairie dogs live underground in communities called towns. At the entrances they make mounds, which serve as tiny lookout towers (30-31). From the top of a mound a prairie dog scans its surroundings for signs of danger. At the sight of a hawk circling overhead or a predator on the ground, the little sentry barks a shrill warning cry. This alerts prairie dogs feeding on the grass nearby. They dash to an entrance and dive underground.

No matter where you live, the world beneath your feet offers a variety of places to explore and plants and animals to discover. To help children learn more about their world, enjoy these activities with them:

Visit the woods and find out what lives under a dead log. Using a strong stick, gently move the log. Look quickly, for many animals scurry away. Under the bark and in the wood you might see smaller animals. Try to leave the log as you found it.

See what creatures live in your own backyard. Place an old sheet on the ground, weight it down with stones, and leave it overnight. In the morning, lift it up and see what has crawled underneath. You should at least find insects, spiders, and sow bugs.

Take a tape recorder with you to a field or to the woods on a summer day. Stand very still and listen. Record the sounds, and try later to identify which animals made them. If you live near a pond, try recording the sounds of frogs and toads in spring. Borrow a record of animal calls from your library to help you identify the species that live all around you.

Make a terrarium to hold such creatures as snails and spiders. Use a glass aquarium, large wide-mouthed jar, or

clear plastic box for the terrarium. From a single place, collect woodland plants that don't grow too tall, such as mosses and low-growing ferns.

Put a two-inch layer of gravel or pebbles mixed with charcoal on the bottom of the terrarium for drainage. Then add soil and carefully set in your plants. Add interesting rocks and pieces of bark as hiding places. Have a piece of glass or clear plastic cut to fit the top of your terrarium, and tape it in place. Keep the top on about half the time, to hold moisture inside. Add water daily by briefly sprinkling the plants. Do not put water in a dish.

If you have a burrowing spider, such as a trap-door spider (27), use a deep wide-mouthed jar for its home and put in plenty of sand and dirt. You can watch it dig and build its burrow home. Feed a spider mealworms, small bugs, crickets, and other insects. To learn what a snail likes, try feeding it lettuce, celery, bits of apple, and insects.

As you watch the animals in your terrarium, try to discover how they move, eat, rest, and react to their environment. With a magnifying glass, watch the snail use its foot as it climbs up the glass. Look for the trail of slime it makes as it moves. After a few days, put your creatures back where you found them. Then try to imagine what it would be like if you lived on or under the ground as these animals do.

ADDITIONAL READING

Discovering the Outdoors, by Laurence Pringle. (N.Y., The Natural History Press, 1969). Ages 12 and under.

Once we went on a picnic, by Aileen Fisher. (N.Y., Thomas Y. Crowell Company, 1975). Ages 5-9.

Secrets of a Wildlife Watcher, by Jim Arnosky. (N.Y., Lothrop, Lee and Shepard, 1983). Ages 8 and up.

Suburban Wildlife, by Richard Headstrom. (Englewood Cliffs, N.J., Prentice-Hall, 1984). Family reading.